SHISTORICAL PERSPECTIVES
In Their Own Words

The Words of CESAR CHAVEZ

Jagger Youssef

PowerKiDS press

Published in 2023 by The Rosen Publishing Group, Inc.
2544 Clinton Street, Buffalo, NY 14224

Portions of this work were originally authored by Sarah Machajewski and published as *Cesar Chavez in His Own Words*. All new material in this edition authored by Jagger Youssef.

Editor: Therese Shea
Book Design: Michael Flynn

Photo Credits: Cover https://commons.wikimedia.org/wiki/File:Cesar_Chavez_40915a.tif; (series background) merrymuuu/Shutterstock.com; (fact box) Miloje/Shutterstock.com; p. 5 https://commons.wikimedia.org/wiki/File:Democratic_Convention_in_New_York_City,_July_14,_1976._Cesar_Chavez_at_podium,_nominating_Gov._Brown.jpg; p. 7 Everett Collection/Shutterstock.com; p. 8 Yarygin/Shuttersock.com; p. 9 Robert Biedermann/Shutterstock.com; p. 11 courtesy of the Library of Congress; p. 13 (Helen and Barack) AP Photo/Carolyn Kaster; p. 13 (Gandhi) https://commons.wikimedia.org/wiki/File:Mahatma-Gandhi,_studio,_1931.jpg; p. 15 courtesy of Walter P. Reuther Library; p. 16 Music4mix/Shutterstock.com; p. 17 (flag) railway fx/Shutterstock.com; p. 17 (UFW logo) https://en.wikipedia.org/wiki/File:UFW_Flag.svg; p. 19 https://en.wikipedia.org/wiki/Cesar_Chavez#/media/File:Cesar_chavez2.jpg; p. 21 AP Photo/Walter Zeboski; p. 23 William Warren/Alamy Stock Photo; p. 25 (all) https://en.wikipedia.org/wiki/File:National_Farm_Workers_Association_protest_buttons.png; p. 27 AP Photo/David F. Smith.

Library of Congress Cataloging-in-Publication Data

Names: Youssef, Jagger, author.
Title: The words of Cesar Chavez / Jagger Youssef.
Description: New York : PowerKids Press, [2023] | Series: Historical perspectives: in their own words | Includes index.
Identifiers: LCCN 2022027974 (print) | LCCN 2022027975 (ebook) | ISBN 9781642824582 (library binding) | ISBN 9781642824568 (paperback) | ISBN 9781642824599 (ebook)
Subjects: LCSH: Chavez, Cesar, 1927-1993--Juvenile literature. | Labor leaders--United States--Biography--Juvenile literature. | Mexican American migrant agricultural laborers--Biography--Juvenile literature. | Agricultural laborers--Labor unions--United States--History--Juvenile literature. | United Farm Workers--History--Juvenile literature.
Classification: LCC HD6509.C48 Y69 2023 (print) | LCC HD6509.C48 (ebook) | DDC 331.88/13092 [B]--dc23/eng/20220623
LC record available at https://lccn.loc.gov/2022027974
LC ebook record available at https://lccn.loc.gov/2022027975

Manufactured in the United States of America

CPSIA Compliance Information: Batch #CWPK23. For further information contact Rosen Publishing at 1-800-237-9932.

CONTENTS

ACTIVIST AGAINST INJUSTICE

Agriculture in the United States has always depended on the hard work of men and women. Even today, with machines handling so much farmwork, certain jobs need to be done by the careful hands of human beings. And unfortunately, though these jobs can require long, backbreaking hours, farmworkers are sometimes not treated well or paid fairly.

Years ago, however, the situation was even worse. One Mexican American in the 1960s rose to become a leader among farm laborers. His voice rallied others to demand better conditions for farmworkers. This **activist** and labor leader, Cesar Chavez, understood their troubles because he, too, toiled on farms as a **migrant** worker. He understood the tiring work and the dangers involved. His nonviolent movement for justice inspired millions and changed lives.

LOOKING BACK

Cesar Chavez took his role as a leader seriously: "There has to be someone who is willing to do it, who is willing to take whatever risks are required."

Primary Sources of History

In telling the story of Cesar Chavez's life and work, his own words are essential to understand him. This book uses primary sources, which are documents or objects created during a time in history. Speeches, letters, interviews, and artwork are primary sources, for example. They help us study history directly through the ideas of people who lived it. Cesar Chavez's own words can tell you about the man himself as well as the farmworkers' movement.

Cesar Chavez became a powerful voice for countless farmworkers who had suffered in silence.

EARLY LIFE

Cesario "Cesar" Estrada Chavez was born in Yuma, Arizona, on March 31, 1927. He was named for his grandfather Cesario, who **immigrated** to the United States from Mexico in 1898. Cesar was the second oldest of the family's six children.

When Cesar was young, his family had enough money to live comfortably. However, an Anglo, or white, landowner cheated his father, and the Chavez family was placed in a bad financial position. At the same time, the Great Depression had descended on the United States. Chavez remembered, "[The Great Depression] . . . meant nothing to me then, but [was] a condition that would deeply scar our lives, despite my father's hard work." Cesar's family didn't have enough money to pay the taxes on their land and business. They lost them both.

LOOKING BACK

Cesar Chavez's parents owned both a ranch and a small grocery store, but lost them during the Great Depression. People everywhere suffered.

The Great Depression

The Great Depression was a period of economic devastation around the world. In October 1929, the U.S. stock market crashed. Banks and businesses lost millions of dollars. By 1933, over 12 million Americans were unemployed. With no work and no money, they were unable to buy food for their families. Millions of families, like Cesar's, lost their homes and their businesses. Many people were forced to move in search of work, leaving behind everything they knew.

During the Great Depression, a lack of rain made life hard for Great Plains farmers. Their land became known as the Dust Bowl. Some moved to California to try to find jobs.

TO CALIFORNIA

After losing their home, the Chavez family moved to California to become migrant workers. Migrant families moved from place to place following crops that were in season. Cesar recalled, "I can't remember our other migrant years as well as the first two. As we moved around, they blurred. The crops changed and we kept moving. There was a time for planting, and a time for thinning, and an endless variety of harvests up and down the state."

Today, more than 90 percent of U.S. lettuce and 99 percent of U.S. grapes are grown in California. Farmworkers are essential to the business of agriculture.

LOOKING BACK

The Chavez family spoke Spanish at home. At school, Cesar wasn't allowed to speak Spanish.

Missing School

Chavez finished eighth grade, but then his father was injured in an accident. He had to start working so his mother didn't have to. "No one had to tell me how bad off we were . . . It was an automatic thing for me to say, 'I'll go to work, and I'll go to high school in two years.' But I never got there . . . It's an economic reason entirely." This was a common fate for migrant children.

His family first lived in Oxnard, California. Then they moved to Pescadero and then a San Jose **barrio** known as Sal Si Puedes, which means "get out if you can" in Spanish. Crowded, dirty, and often lacking electricity or running water, conditions in these places were poor. In the 1940s, the family settled in Delano, California.

DIFFICULT WORK

The life of a migrant worker wasn't an easy one. Picking crops can be exhausting. Chavez knew and spoke out about its physical effects. He remembered the skin on his hands splitting from picking crops, back pain, sore fingers, and more. Workers were exposed to **pesticides** and extreme heat. "Many things in farm labor are terrible," he said. "They should find a way of doing this work that will leave the human being whole."

Workers were paid by the number of crops picked or acres covered, so they worked quickly. But they weren't paid much. In 1933, some growers offered 60 cents for picking 100 pounds (45 kg) of cotton. Chavez tried to find ways to make work easier and faster for his family. "We had to [finish] that acre," he said.

LOOKING BACK

Chavez had attended 38 schools by the time he finished the eighth grade. By the age of 15, he was a full-time migrant worker.

A Poor Plan

In 1942, an **executive order** called the Mexican Farm Labor Program launched the Bracero Program. The program brought more than 4 million Mexican farmworkers to the United States. But white growers took advantage of Mexican laborers, paying them less than white workers. Mexican laborers often didn't understand their contracts, which were written in English. Many were forced to return to Mexico when these contracts expired. Some blame the Bracero Program for human rights abuses. It was discontinued in 1964.

Mexican laborers pick sugar beets in California in 1943.

A DIFFERENT KIND OF EDUCATION

Chavez served in the U.S. Navy from 1946 to 1948. When he returned home, he married Helen Favela, and they eventually settled in the Sal Si Puedes barrio of San Jose. Together they had eight children.

Chavez met Father Donald McDonnell, a priest at the local Catholic church. "My education started when I met Father McDonnell," Chavez said. Through McDonnell, Chavez learned about St. Francis of Assisi, who was a champion of the poor, and Mahatma Gandhi, who used nonviolence as a force for change. Later, when Chavez became an activist, he kept these men's actions in mind. McDonnell and Chavez also talked of the injustices farmworkers faced, unfair legislation, economics, and the striking difference between how workers and growers lived.

LOOKING BACK

Chavez wrote, "When we apply Gandhi's philosophy of nonviolence, it really forces us to think, really forces us to work hard. But it has power. It attracts the support of the people."

Gandhi and Civil Disobedience

Civil disobedience is refusing to obey rules and laws in a nonviolent way. This means using methods that don't hurt people–such as **sit-ins**, protests, **boycotts**, and fasts–to achieve change. This philosophy was made famous by Mahatma Gandhi, a man who used nonviolent resistance in the first half of the 20th century to help end British rule in India. His teachings inspired many activists in the United States, including Chavez.

Mahatma Gandhi

Family and faith were important to Cesar Chavez. His wife Helen, above, also became an activist.

FRED ROSS

When Chavez was 25 years old, he met another person who had a major impact on his life. Fred Ross was a leader of the Los Angeles area Community Service Organization (CSO), a group that worked on behalf of Mexican Americans. It fought racism and helped Mexicans immigrate. The CSO also helped thousands of Mexican Americans gain citizenship, register to vote, and fought **discrimination**.

Ross came to San Jose to set up a chapter of the CSO. Chavez sometimes worked 15 hours a day registering people to vote. As Chavez listened to Ross, he became inspired: "[Ross] did such a good job of explaining how poor people could build power that I could even taste it . . . I saw him organize, and I wanted to learn."

LOOKING BACK

When he met Fred Ross, Chavez was a farmworker in apricot orchards outside of San Jose.

First Fight

Chavez described voter registration for the CSO as his "first fight with this power structure." Political groups in California put rules in place that said organizers could only register voters during daylight hours. They couldn't work on Sundays and couldn't speak Spanish when they were registering. On voting days, the political groups used **intimidation** at the polls. These actions made it difficult for Mexican Americans to vote.

Fred Ross left San Jose in 1953. Chavez became the CSO's national director in 1958.

ENTER THE NFWA

Chavez's work with the CSO made him aware of the widespread problems of migrant workers. They were often desperately poor, couldn't understand English, and lacked the tools to organize themselves. Chavez thought he could organize a **labor union** that worked on their behalf. This organization would fight for better wages and working conditions. It would also offer social services to its members. Chavez brought the labor union idea to the CSO, but they rejected it. In 1962, he left the organization.

Chavez cofounded the National Farm Workers Association (NFWA) with Dolores Huerta, another former CSO organizer. Chavez and Huerta worked tirelessly to grow their union. Chavez received no pay until the NFWA had enough money to operate. By 1964, it had 1,000 members.

Dolores Huerta

Resigning

Chavez found that he disagreed with some CSO methods. He asked for change through his words and actions: "I refused to sit at the head table at meetings, refused to wear a suit and tie . . . At every meeting I got up and gave my standard speech: we shouldn't meet in fancy motels, we were getting away from the people, farmworkers had to be organized. But nothing happened. In March of '62 I resigned."

LOOKING BACK

By 1964, the NFWA had an insurance program, a **credit union**, and a newspaper.

The NFWA used a black eagle as its symbol. The eagle symbolized the pride and dignity of its workers. The black eagle was designed so that workers could draw it on homemade flags.

THE GRAPE STRIKE

Through the NFWA, Chavez tried to correct what he believed were mistakes in the CSO's organization. In 1965, workers on a rose farm asked the NFWA to help them strike. It resulted in a large increase in pay for the workers.

In September 1965, the Agricultural Workers Organizing Committee (AWOC), a union popular with Filipino American farmworkers, launched a strike when Delano grape growers cut wages during the harvest. Growers asked NFWA workers to take their place. Instead, Chavez's union voted to join the strike.

In 1966, Chavez said, "It is bigger . . . than just a strike. And if this spirit grows within the farm labor movement, one day we can use the force that we have to help correct a lot of things that are wrong in this society."

LOOKING BACK

How much did farmworkers earn back then? The migrant workers who started the grape strike were earning $1.25 per hour. They wanted $1.40 per hour.

Striking Back

A strike is a form of protest. Employees refuse to work for an employer, usually in order to gain something. Striking can be effective. When people strike, work may stop and employers lose money. Employees lose out on money too. Strikers often form lines in front of their place of employment, holding signs and declaring what they want. Sometimes, strikes are met with violence. The NFWA was committed to staying nonviolent, even when they were threatened.

Grape growers brought in strikebreakers—sometimes called scabs—to work while the strike continued. NFWA members often convinced them to leave the fields, and many ended up joining the cause.

THE STRENGTH OF NONVIOLENCE

Chavez needed the public's support for the Delano grape strike to work. His leadership style and insistence on nonviolence did just that. When people saw strikers not fight back, even when they were attacked and hurt, they became sympathetic. "Nonviolence has the power to attract people and to generate power," Chavez said. "By and large, people oppose violence. So when government or growers use violence against us, we strategize around it. We can respond nonviolently, because that swings people to our side, and that gives us our strength."

Chavez invited other people to join in the strike. Hundreds of students, church groups, activist organizations, and everyday people answered the call. In a few years, the Delano grape strike had national support.

LOOKING BACK

In 1966, the NFWA merged with the Agricultural Workers Organizing Committee to form the United Farm Workers Organizing Committee.

Getting to the Goal

While some growers agreed to increase wages, Chavez's main goal was to unionize laborers. A union could bring change across farms. Most importantly, a union could secure a contract for better wages and working conditions. However, growers rejected this idea. In a speech during the strike, Chavez proclaimed, "Our strike will stop every way the grower makes money until we have a union contract that guarantees us a fair share of the money he makes from our work!"

To bring attention to the Delano strike, Chavez organized a march in March 1966 from Delano to Sacramento, California's capital city—a distance of about 280 miles (450 km).

A FAMOUS BOYCOTT

Chavez proved he had the nation's attention and sympathy when the union called for a grape boycott. People across the country were encouraged to stop buying grapes that didn't have a union label to show their support for farmworkers. If people didn't buy grapes, growers wouldn't make money. Growers would be forced to **negotiate**.

The grape boycott proved that even the smallest action could lead to great change. It brought the farmworkers' cause into millions of people's homes. Some union dockworkers in California refused to load non-union grapes, letting them rot, to show their support too.

"To us the boycott of grapes was the most near-perfect of nonviolent struggles. The boycott demonstrated to the whole country, the whole world, what people can do by nonviolent action," Chavez said.

LOOKING BACK

In 1969, Chavez was on the cover of *Time* magazine. At its peak, over 14 million Americans supported the grape boycott.

Chavez Fasts

In 1968, Chavez began a 25-day water-only fast as a peaceful protest. People urged him to eat. But for Chavez, social justice could only be won through personal sacrifice. At the end of his fast, too weak to speak, he issued a statement: "I am convinced that the truest act of courage . . . is to sacrifice ourselves for others in a totally nonviolent struggle for justice. To be a man is to suffer for others."

Chavez agreed to end his fast on March 10, 1968. He invited Senator Robert F. Kennedy to join him.

THE STRIKE ENDS

After five years of growing pressure, more than 25 Delano grape growers finally agreed to sign contracts with the United Farm Workers Organizing Committee union. The strike officially ended in July 1970. The union contracts guaranteed higher wages, health insurance benefits, and better working conditions for farm laborers.

Chavez also succeeded in another way. His efforts made people aware of the inequalities migrant workers faced. It was a step in the direction of changing how society operated. In an interview conducted in 1970, Chavez was asked what it would take to achieve the kind of society he envisioned. He said, "It isn't the rule or the procedure or the **ideology**, but it's human beings that will make it."

LOOKING BACK

In 1971, the United Farm Workers Organizing Committee became the United Farm Workers of America (UFW).

Finally, a Voice

The Delano grape strike had helped thousands of migrant workers, but it also helped Mexican Americans as a whole, a group that experienced much discrimination. As Chavez emerged as a powerful leader and activist, he empowered all Hispanics to have a voice. Mexican Americans rallied around the union that worked on their behalf. They had voting power and political weight. Chavez awoke a wave of activism. Since Chavez's time, thousands of Hispanic leaders have held public office.

The farmworkers had not only been the victims of growers. Law enforcement officials had arrested some without cause. Some workers had the water supply shut off at their homes as revenge.

THE NEXT FIGHT

The UFW's work wasn't done as long as farmworkers were unfairly treated. In 1972, California lettuce growers entered into a deal with the Western Conference of Teamsters union in which the Teamsters agreed to represent lettuce pickers. However, the workers had no say in the matter. They didn't choose this representation, and the Teamsters didn't work for their best interests. Workers were angry.

Chavez and the UFW took action. They organized workers who wanted to unionize on their own. They called for a lettuce boycott and encouraged a strike. In 1975, a landmark law passed in California greatly helped the cause. The state's Agricultural Labor Relations Act granted farm laborers the right to collective bargaining, which means meetings between an employer and the leaders of a union to settle how workers will be treated.

LOOKING BACK

During what was called the "Salad Bowl Strike," over 5,000 workers walked off the job. It was the largest farmworker strike in American history.

Powerful Slogan

In 1972, Arizona passed a law that prevented farmworkers from striking or boycotting during harvests. The governor said, "As far as I'm concerned, those people don't exist." Chavez began another fast. A group of leaders visited Chavez as he lay weak in his bed. They told him lawmakers and growers were too powerful to fight. "It can't be done," they said. Dolores Huerta, standing by Chavez, responded: "¡Si, si se puede!" which meant "Yes, yes we can!" The UFW adopted the saying.

In 1977, the Teamsters agreed to end its efforts to represent the farmworkers. The UFW signed contracts with growers.

A LIFE OF SERVICE

Cesar Chavez and the UFW continued to answer the call of farmworkers who needed aid. In the 1980s, Chavez brought attention to the use of pesticides on grapes, linking them to health problems in workers and consumers. In 1988, he held a 36-day fast, damaging his health. He died in Arizona in 1993 at the age of 66. UFW president Arturo Rodriguez said, "Cesar gave his last ounce of strength defending the farmworkers." More than 35,000 people attended his funeral.

During his life, Chavez called on all people to do what they can to support just causes. He stated, "Once social change begins, it cannot be reversed. You cannot uneducate the person who has learned to read. You cannot humiliate the person who feels pride. And you cannot oppress the people who are not afraid anymore."

LOOKING BACK

In 1994, President Bill Clinton awarded Cesar Chavez the Presidential Medal of Freedom, which is the highest civilian honor in the United States. Cesar's wife Helen accepted it.

Honors

Cesar Chavez is the most honored labor organizer in U.S. history. His birthday, March 31, is a state holiday in three states: California, Colorado, and Texas. Los Angeles renamed a street Cesar E. Chavez Avenue. Statues are dedicated to him. San Francisco, California, observes the Cesar Chavez Day Parade in April. Cities have parks named for him, and several schools across the nation are named for him too. His name and his work live on.

Timeline of Cesar Chavez's Life

1927 Cesar Chavez is born near Yuma, Arizona, on March 31.

1929 The Great Depression hits the United States.

1938 The Chavez family moves from Arizona to California.

1946 Chavez joins the U.S. Navy.

1948 Chavez meets Father Donald McDonnell.

1952 Chavez meets Fred Ross and joins the Community Service Organization (CSO).

1958 Chavez becomes the director of the CSO.

1965 The Delano grape strike begins.

1968 Chavez fasts for the first time in support of the strike.

1970 Grape growers agree to union contracts.
Chavez and the United Farm Workers of America (UFW) call for a boycott of California lettuce.

1975 California's Agricultural Labor Relations Act grants farmworkers the right to collective bargaining.

1987 Chavez calls for a nationwide boycott of grapes to protest pesticides.

1993 Chavez dies in Arizona.

GLOSSARY

activist: One who stresses direct action to support or oppose one side of an issue.

barrio: A Spanish-speaking part of a town or city.

boycott: The refusal to buy something or do something as a protest.

credit union: A nonprofit association where members save money and take out loans at lower interest rates.

discrimination: The practice of unfairly treating a person or group of people.

executive order: A declaration by the president or a governor that has the force of law.

ideology: A set of beliefs, values, and ideas that shape an individual.

immigrate: To come to live permanently in a foreign country.

intimidation: The act of frightening someone in order to make them do what you want.

labor union: A group of workers that join together to argue for better benefits.

migrant: A person who goes from one place to another often to find work.

negotiate: To discuss something formally in order to make an agreement.

pesticide: A substance used for destroying bugs or other creatures that are harmful to plants or animals.

sit-in: A protest in which people sit or stay in a place and refuse to leave.

FOR MORE INFORMATION

Books

Blas, Terry. *Who Was the Voice of the People? Cesar Chavez.* New York, NY: Penguin Workshop, 2021.

Cipriano, Jeri. *Cesar Chavez: Friend to Farm Workers*. Egremont, MA: Red Chair Press, 2021.

Mattern, Joanne. *Cesar Chavez: Labor Rights Activist*. New York, NY: Cavendish Square Publishing, 2020.

Websites

Amazing Americans: Cesar Chavez
www.americaslibrary.gov/aa/chavez/aa_chavez_subj.html
The Library of Congress offers a brief biography of Cesar Chavez as well as links to the biographies of other activists.

Cesar Chavez
westportlibrary.libguides.com/cesarchavez
The Westport Library provides links and videos about Chavez's life.

The Story of Cesar Chavez
ufw.org/research/history/story-cesar-chavez/
The United Farm Workers have more details about Chavez's life and impact.

Publisher's note to educators and parents: Our editors have carefully reviewed these websites to ensure that they are suitable for students. Many websites change frequently, however, and we cannot guarantee that a site's future contents will continue to meet our high standards of quality and educational value. Be advised that students should be closely supervised whenever they access the internet.

INDEX